MW00626708

1

"If thou wilt diligently hearken to the voice of the Lord thy God, and wilt do that which is right in His sight, and wilt give ear to His commandments, and keep all His statutes, I will put none of these diseases upon thee, which I have brought upon the Egyptians: for I am the Lord that healeth thee."

-Exodus 15:26

Obedience Qualifies You For A Miracle.

-MIKE MURDOCK

2

"There shall no evil befall thee, neither shall any plague come nigh thy dwelling."

–Psalm 91:10

The Proof of Love Is The Desire To Protect.

-MIKE MURDOCK

3

"He sent His Word, and healed them, and delivered them from their destructions."

-Psalm 107:20

The Word You Believe Determines The Healing You Receive. -MIKE MURDOCK

4

"But He was wounded for our transgressions, He was bruised for our iniquities: the chastisement of our peace was upon Him; and with His stripes we are healed."

-Isaiah 53:5

Your Need Decides His Gift.

-MIKE MURDOCK

5

"Bless the Lord, O my soul, and forget not all His benefits: Who forgiveth all thine iniquities; Who healeth all thy diseases."

–Psalm 103:2-3

Those Who Remember Are Always Thankful.

-MIKE MURDOCK

6

"The thief cometh not, but for to steal, and to kill, and to destroy: I am come that they might have life, and that they might have it more abundantly."

–John 10:10

The Purpose of Relationship Is Increase.

-MIKE MURDOCK

7

"Therefore I say unto you, What things soever ye desire, when ye pray, believe that ye receive them, and ye shall have them."

-Mark 11:24

Asking Is The Beginning of Receiving.

-MIKE MURDOCK

8

"Is any sick among you? let him call for the elders of the church; and let them pray over him, anointing him with oil in the name of the Lord: And the prayer of faith shall save the sick, and the Lord shall raise him up; and if he have committed sins, they shall be forgiven him."

–James 5:14-15

The Instruction You Follow Decides The Miracle You Receive. *-MIKE MURDOCK*

9

"Who His own self bare our sins in His own body on the tree, that we, being dead to sins, should live unto right-eousness: by Whose stripes ye were healed."

−1 Peter 2:24

If Time Heals, The Crucifixion Was Unnecessary.

-MIKE MURDOCK

10

"Ye are of God, little children, and have overcome them: because greater is He that is in you, than he that is in the world."

– 1 John 4:4

The Power Within You Can Cure The Pain Within You.

-MIKE MURDOCK

11

"Beloved, I wish above all things that thou mayest prosper and be in health, even as thy soul prospereth."

-3 John 2

The Word of God Is
The Will of God.

-MIKE MURDOCK

12

"Every good gift and every perfect gift is from above, and cometh down from the Father of lights, with Whom is no variableness, neither shadow of turning."

–James 1:17

The Quality of The Gift Reveals The Character of The Giver. -MIKE MURDOCK

13

"Jesus Christ the same yesterday, and to day, and for ever."

-Hebrews 13:8

He's Done It Once;
He's Done It Twice
And He Can Do It Again.

-MIKE MURDOCK

14

"Behold, the Lord's hand is not shortened, that it cannot save; neither His ear heavy, that it cannot hear."

–Isaiah 59:1

You Are Never As Far From A Miracle As It First Appears.

-MIKE MURDOCK

15

"Then shall thy light break forth as the morning, and thine health shall spring forth speedily: and thy righteousness shall go before thee; the glory of the Lord shall be thy rereward."

–Isaiah 58:8

Your Faith Decides
Your Seasons.

-MIKE MURDOCK

16

"So shall My Word be that goeth forth out of My mouth: it shall not return unto Me void, but it shall accomplish that which I please, and it shall prosper in the thing whereto I sent it."

–Isaiah 55:11

The Word of God Within You Is The Power of God Within You. *-MIKE MURDOCK*

17

"And ye shall serve the Lord your God, and He shall bless thy bread, and thy water; and I will take sickness away from the midst of thee."

–Exodus 23:25

The Quality of Your Servanthood Determines The Quality of Your Rewards. *-MIKE MURDOCK*

18

"But without faith it is impossible to please Him: for he that cometh to God must believe that He is, and that He is a rewarder of them that diligently seek Him."

–Hebrews 11:6

God's Only Pain Is To Be Doubted; His Only Pleasure Is To Be Believed.

-MIKE MURDOCK

19

"Verily I say unto you, Whatsoever ye shall bind on earth shall be bound in Heaven: and whatsoever ye shall loose on earth shall be loosed in Heaven."

–Matthew 18:18

What You Do First Determines What God Will Do Second.

-MIKE MURDOCK

20

"...When the enemy shall come in like a flood, the Spirit of the Lord shall lift up a standard against him."

–Isaiah 59:19

Someone You Cannot See Is The Enemy You Must Defeat.

-MIKE MURDOCK

21

"A merry heart doeth good like a medicine: but a broken spirit drieth the bones."

–Proverbs 17:22

The Atmosphere You Create Determines The Healing You Unleash.   -MIKE MURDOCK

22

"But unto you that fear My name shall the Sun of right-eousness arise with healing in His wings."

–Malachi 4:2

What You Respect You Will Attract.
-MIKE MURDOCK

23

"Trust in the Lord with all thine heart; and lean not unto thine own understanding."

–Proverbs 3:5

The Proof of Trust Is The Willingness To Wait.

-MIKE MURDOCK

24

"...Ask, and it shall be given you; seek, and ye shall find; knock, and it shall be opened unto you."

-Luke 11:9

The Proof of Faith Is Pursuit.

-MIKE MURDOCK

25

"No weapon that is formed against thee shall prosper; and every tongue that shall rise against thee in judgment thou shalt condemn. This is the heritage of the servants of the Lord, and their righteousness is of Me, saith the Lord."

–Isaiah 54:17

Submission To Authority Qualifies You For Protection, Provision And Promotion.

-MIKE MURDOCK

26

"I shall not die, but live, and declare the works of the Lord."

–Psalm 118:17

The Seasons of Your Life Will Change Every Time You Decide To Use Your Faith.

-MIKE MURDOCK

27

"My son, attend to My words; incline thine ear unto My sayings. For they are life unto those that find them, and health to all their flesh."

–Proverbs 4:20, 22

What Enters You Determines What Exits You.

-MIKE MURDOCK

28

"For I will restore health unto thee, and I will heal thee of thy wounds, saith the Lord."

–Jeremiah 30:17

**The Author Writes.
The Singer Sings.
The Healer Heals.**
-MIKE MURDOCK

29

"Jesus said unto him, If thou canst believe, all things are possible to him that believeth."

–Mark 9:23

The World Around You Is A Portrait of Your Faith.

-MIKE MURDOCK

30

"O Lord my God, I cried unto Thee, and Thou hast healed me."

–Psalm 30:2

The Willingness To Reach Is The Proof of Faith.

-MIKE MURDOCK

31

"Let us therefore come boldly unto the throne of grace, that we may obtain mercy, and find grace to help in time of need."

–Hebrews 4:16

Miracles Do Not Go Where They Are Needed—Miracles Go Where They Are Pursued.

-MIKE MURDOCK

DECISION

Will You Accept Jesus As Your Personal Savior Today?

The Bible says, "That if thou shalt confess with thy mouth the Lord Jesus, and shalt believe in thine heart that God hath raised Him from the dead, thou shalt be saved," (Romans 10:9).

Pray this prayer from your heart today!

"Dear Jesus, I believe that You died for me and rose again on the third day. I confess I am a sinner...I need Your love and forgiveness...Come into my heart. Forgive my sins. I receive Your eternal life. Confirm Your love by giving me peace, joy and supernatural love for others. Amen."

❏ Yes, Mike, I made a decision to accept Christ as my personal Savior today. Please send me my free gift of your book, *"31 Keys to a New Beginning"* to help me with my new life in Christ.

Name _____ Birthdate _____

Address _____

City _____ State _____ Zip _____

Phone (____) _____ E-Mail _____

Mail To:

The Wisdom Center · 4051 Denton Hwy. · Ft. Worth, TX 76117
1-817-759-BOOK · 1-817-759-2665 · 1-817-759-0300
MikeMurdockBooks.com

Unless otherwise indicated, all Scripture quotations are taken from the King James Version of the Bible.
The Memory Bible On Healing
ISBN 1-56394-239-9/B-196
Copyright © 2003 by MIKE MURDOCK
All publishing rights belong exclusively to Wisdom International
Publisher/Editor: Deborah Murdock Johnson
Published by The Wisdom Center · 4051 Denton Hwy. · Ft. Worth, TX 76117
1-817-759-BOOK · 1-817-759-2665 · 1-817-759-0300
MikeMurdockBooks.com

Clip and Mail

Miracle 7 BOOK PAK!

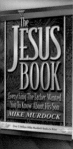

DR. MIKE MURDOCK

① **Dream Seeds** (Book/B-11/106pg/$12)

② **7 Hidden Keys to Favor** (Book/B-119/32pg/$7)

③ **Seeds of Wisdom on Miracles** (Book/B-15/32pg/$5)

④ **Seeds of Wisdom on Prayer** (Book/B-23/32pg/$5)

⑤ **The Jesus Book** (Book/B-27/166pg/$10)

⑥ **The Memory Bible on Miracles** (Book/B-208/32pg/$5)

⑦ **The Mentor's Manna on Attitude** (Book/B-58/32pg/$5)

*Each Wisdom Book may be purchased separately if so desired.

The Wisdom Center
**Miracle 7
Book Pak!**
Only $**30** $49 Value
WBL-24
Wisdom Is The Principal Thing

Add 20% For S/H

Quantity Prices Available Upon Request

THE WISDOM CENTER
4051 Denton Highway · Fort Worth, TX 76117

1-817-759-BOOK
1-817-759-2665
1-817-759-0300

You Will Love Our Website..!
MikeMurdockBooks.com

A

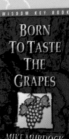

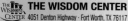

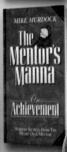

Unforgettable Woman 4
Book Pak!

Seeds Of Wisdom On The Secret Place · Volume 13

Where Miracles Are Born

Secrets of the Journey

MIKE MURDOCK
THE WISDOM FOR WOMEN SERIES

THIRTY-ONE SECRETS of an UNFORGETTABLE WOMAN

Master Secrets from the life of Ruth

THE PROVERBS 31 Woman

MIKE MURDOCK
A 31 DAY MENTORSHIP PROGRAM OF WISDOM

LEADERSHIP SECRETS FOR BALANCE & INCREASE

6

MURDOCK

❶ **Where Miracles Are Born** (Book/B-115/32pg/$7)

❷ **Secrets of The Journey, Vol. 6** (Book/B-102/32pg/$5)

❸ **Thirty-One Secrets of an Unforgettable Woman** (Book/B-57/140pg/$12)

❹ **The Proverbs 31 Woman** (Book/B-49/70pg/$7)

Wisdom Book may be purchased separately if so desired.

The Wisdom Center
Unforgettable Woman 4 Book Pak!
Only $20
$31 Value
PAK-31
Wisdom Is The Principal Thing

Add 20% For S/H

THE WISDOM CENTER
4051 Denton Highway · Fort Worth, TX 76117

1-817-759-BOOK
1-817-759-2665
1-817-759-0300

— You Will Love Our Website..! —
MikeMurdockBooks.com

E

Millionaire-Talk

DR. MIKE MURDOCK

31 Things You Will Need To Become A Millionaire (2-CD's/SOWL-116)

Topics Include:

- You Will Need Financial Heroes
- Your Willingness To Negotiate Everything
- You Must Have The Ability To Transfer Your Enthusiasm, Your Vision To Others
- Know Your Competition
- Be Willing To Train Your Team Personally As To Your Expectations
- Hire Professionals To Do A Professional's Job

I have asked the Lord for 3,000 special partners who will sow an extra Seed of $58 towards ou
Television Outreach Ministry. Your Seed is so appreciated! Remember to request your Gift CD'
2 Disc Volume, *31 Things You Will Need To Become A Millionaire,* when you write this week!

F THE WISDOM CENTER
4051 Denton Highway · Fort Worth, TX 76117

1-817-759-BOOK
1-817-759-2665
1-817-759-0300

You Will Love Our Website..!
MikeMurdockBooks.com